thank you

"I would like to express my heartfelt gratitude to all the readers who have supported and embraced my coloring book."

Introducing "Happy Pups Coloring" – a delightful coloring book designed to bring smiles and spread positivity while allowing you to color adorable, cheerful puppy illustrations.

Are you looking for a fun and uplifting activity that can brighten your day and bring joy to others? Look no further! Immerse yourself in the world of "Happy Pups Coloring" and experience the joy of coloring while sharing positive messages with people around you.

This heartwarming coloring book features a collection of lovable puppies, each captured in moments of pure happiness. As you bring these playful pups to life with your coloring skills, you'll not only enjoy a creative and relaxing experience but also have the opportunity to convey positive messages to those who see your artwork.

Each page of "Happy Pups Coloring" is carefully designed to inspire positivity and optimism. Alongside the endearing puppy illustrations, you'll find uplifting quotes and affirmations that will brighten your spirits and leave you feeling motivated and encouraged. It's a wonderful way to spread positivity and share smiles with friends, family, and even strangers.

Whether you're an experienced colorist or new to coloring, "Happy Pups Coloring" is perfect for everyone. The pages are printed on high-quality paper, ensuring your colors stay vibrant and the artwork can be cherished for years to come.

Join the joyful journey of coloring and spreading positivity with "Happy Pups Coloring." Get your copy today and let these adorable puppies bring laughter, happiness, and positive messages into your life and the lives of others.

With Love

Jennifer Young So

Jennifer Young

INSPIRED INNOVATOR

THE TABLE OF CONTENTS
OF DOG ILLUSTRATIONS IN
THE COLORING BOOK
"HAPPY PUPS COLORING"

1. Dog
2. Cat
3. Horse
4. Elephant
5. Dolphin
6. Lion
7. Tiger
8. Giraffe
9. Monkey
10. Penguin
11. Koala
12. Bear
13. Cheetah
14. Kangaroo
15. Gorilla
16. Wolf
17. Panda
18. Zebra
19. Owl
20. Fox

21. Rabbit
22. Deer
23. Orca
24. Shark
25. Whale
26. Chimpanzee
27. Squirrel
28. Otter
29. Octopus
30. Parrot
31. Turtle
32. Crocodile
33. Seal
34. Hedgehog
35. Camel
36. Raccoon
37. Peacock
38. Sloth
39. Flamingo
40. Meerkat

41. Jellyfish
42. Lobster
43. Eagle
44. Swan
45. Ostrich
46. Rhinoceros
47. Hippopotamus
48. Bison
49. Tarantula
50. Komodo Dragon
51. Scorpion
52. Platypus
53. Armadillo
54. Walrus
55. Bat
56. Gazelle
57. Antelope
58. Llama
59. Alligator
60. Wolverine
61. Hyena
62. Manta Ray
63. Boar
64. Moose
65. Reindeer
66. Hamster
67. Chameleon
68. Snail
69. Rattlesnake
70. Alpaca

71. Tapir
72. Baboon
73. Tasmanian Devil
74. Lemur
75. Dingo
76. Woodpecker
77. Seahorse
78. Stingray
79. Crocodile
80. Ocelot
81. Porcupine
82. Bobcat
83. Macaw
84. Tamarin
85. Manatee
86. Puffin
87. Narwhal
88. Chinchilla
89. Jaguar
90. Falcon
91. Wombat
92. Gila Monster
93. Quokka
94. Capybara
95. Angelfish
96. Box Turtle
97. Caracal
98. Wallaby
99. Axolotl
100. Bonobo

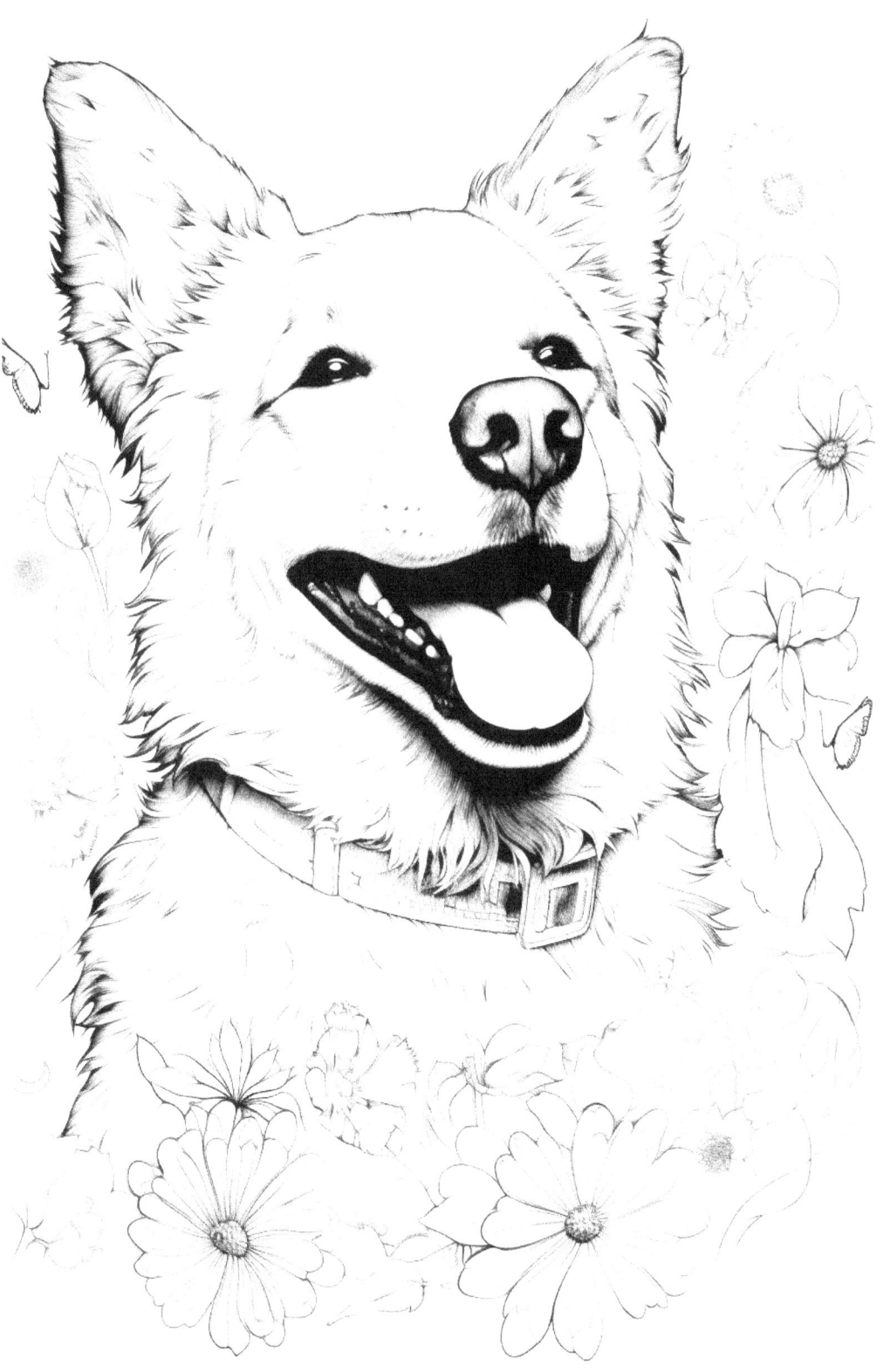

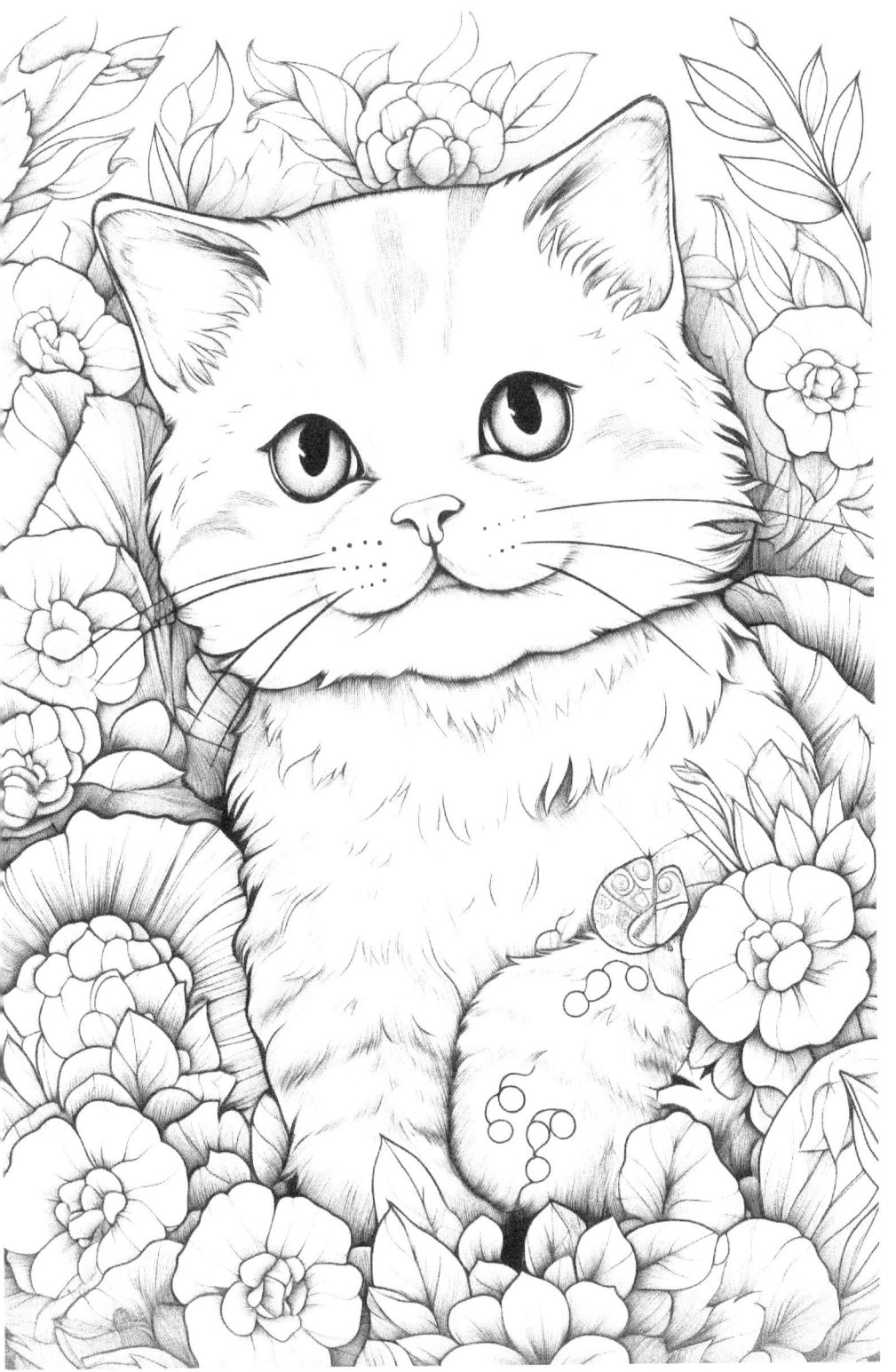

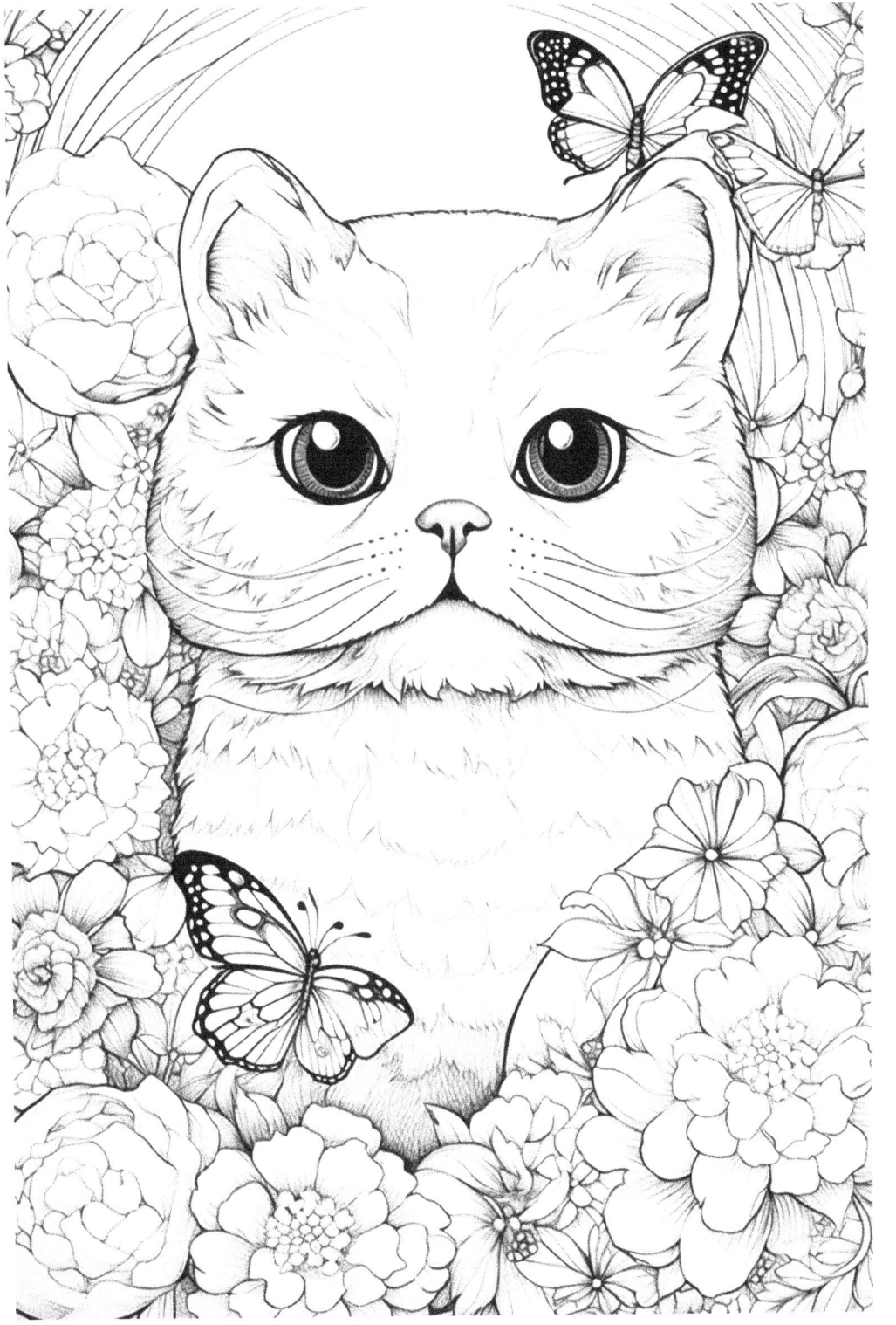

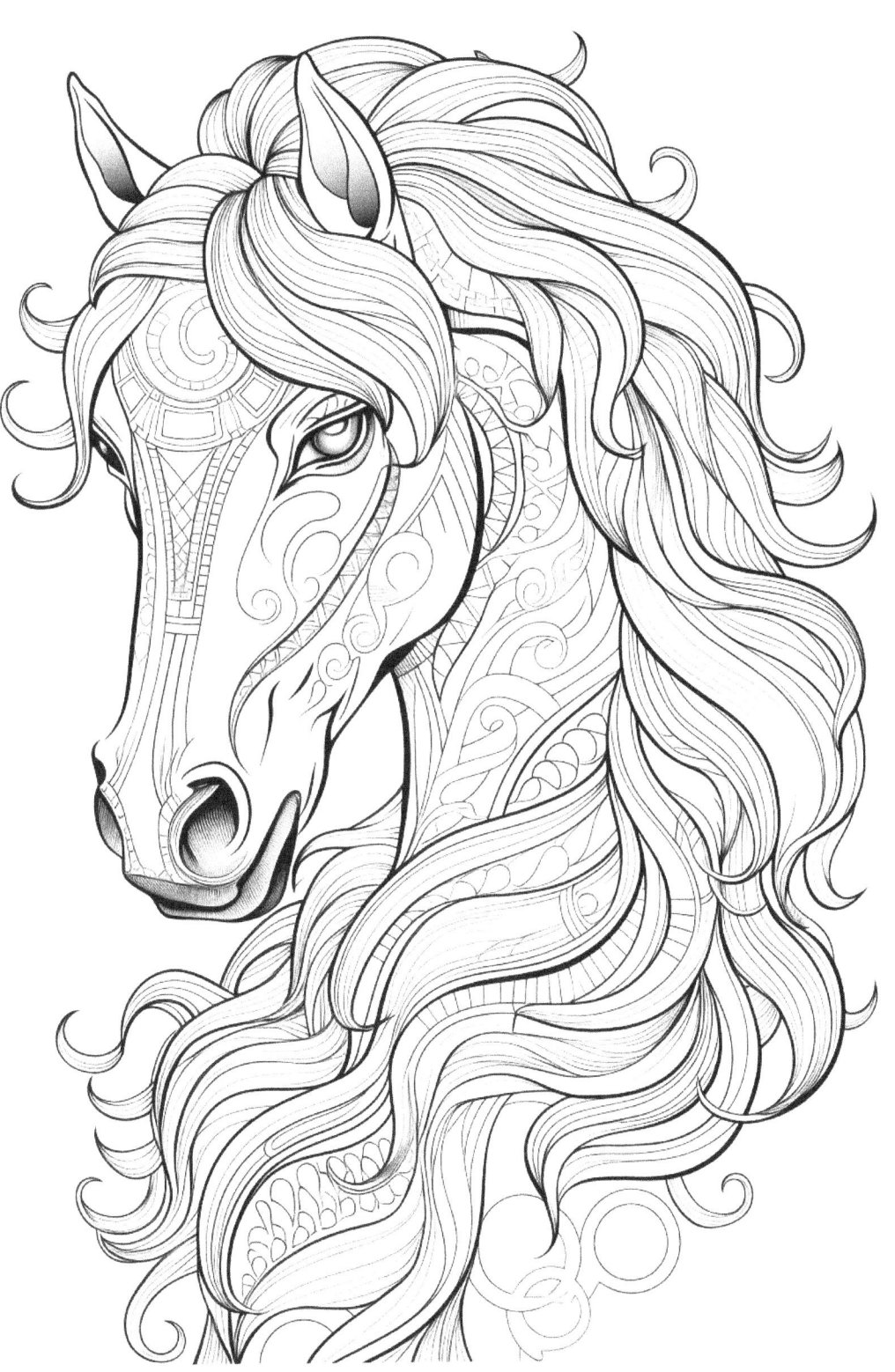

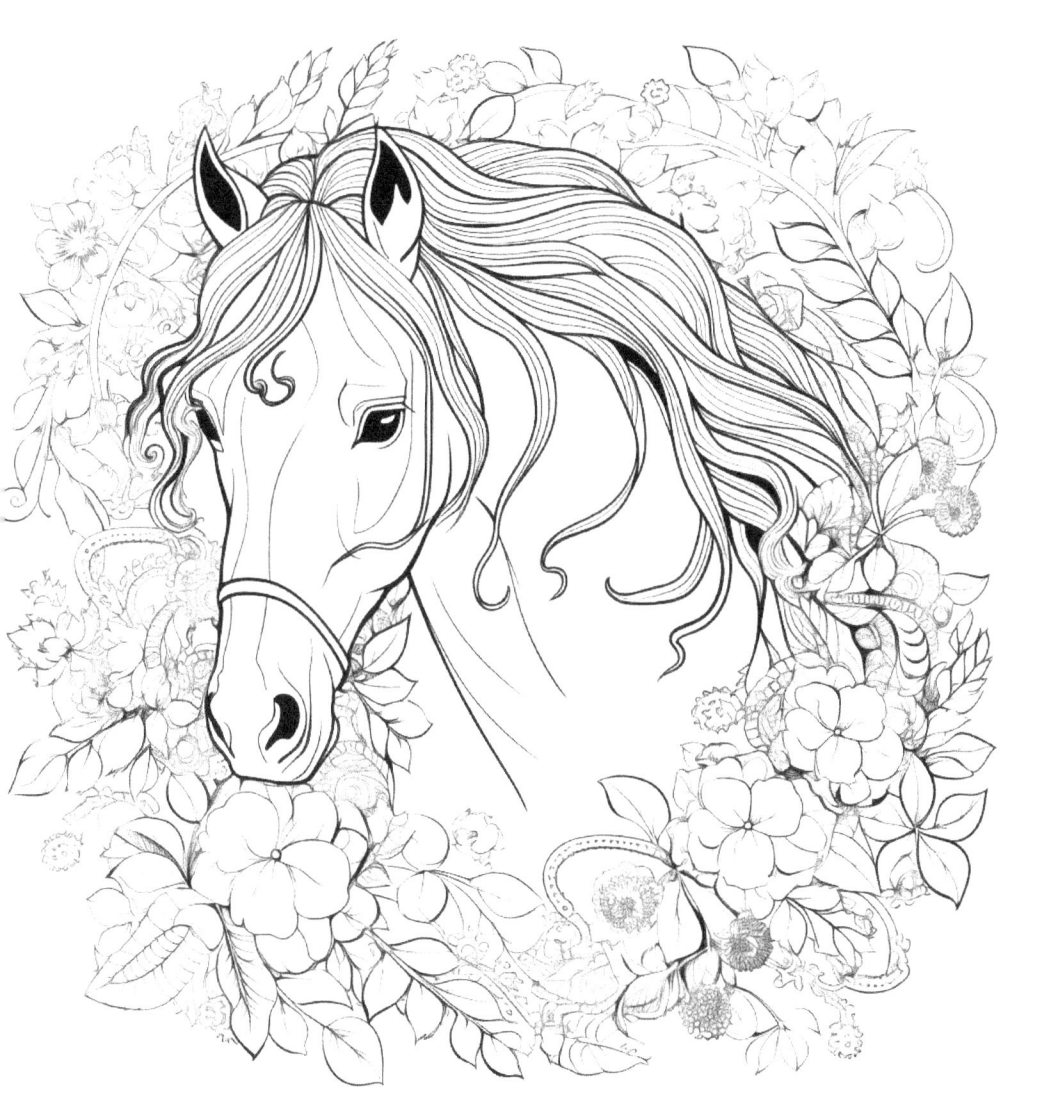

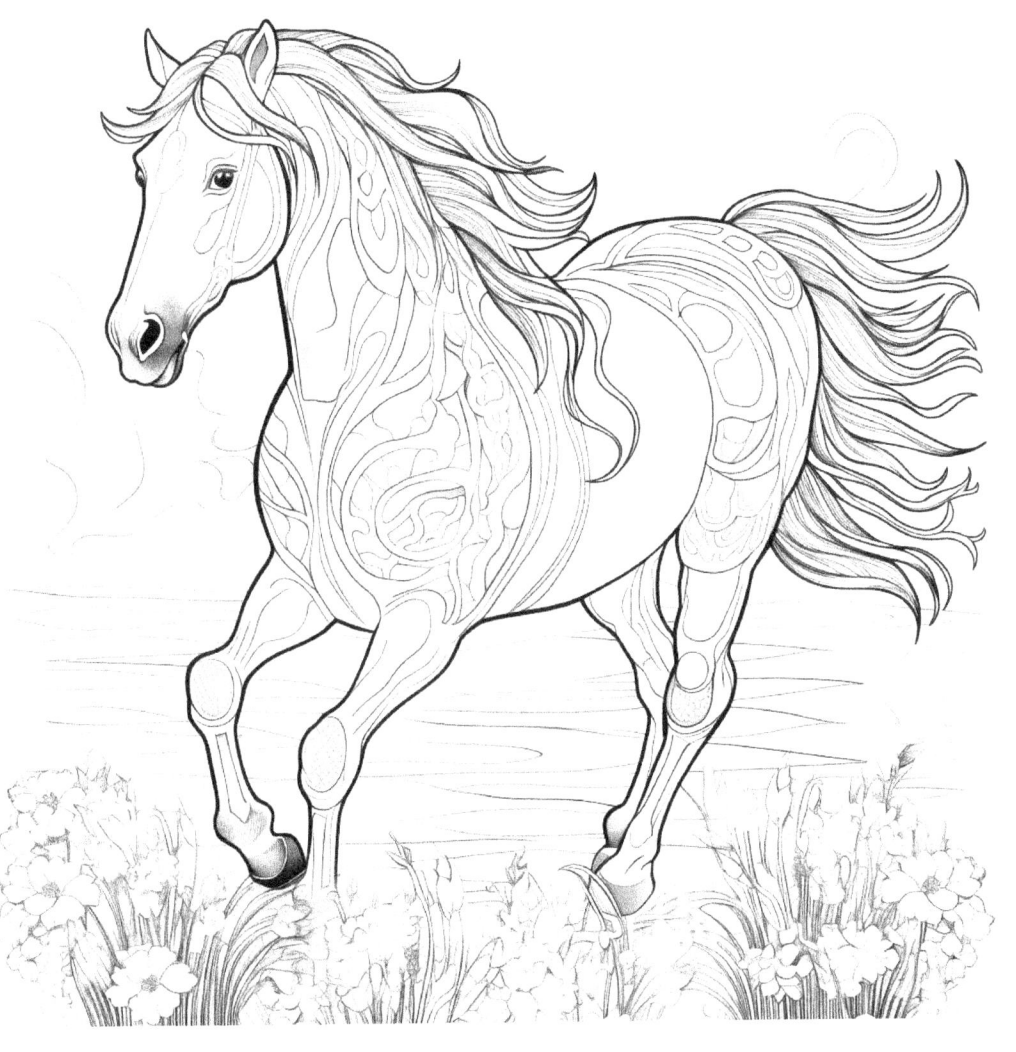

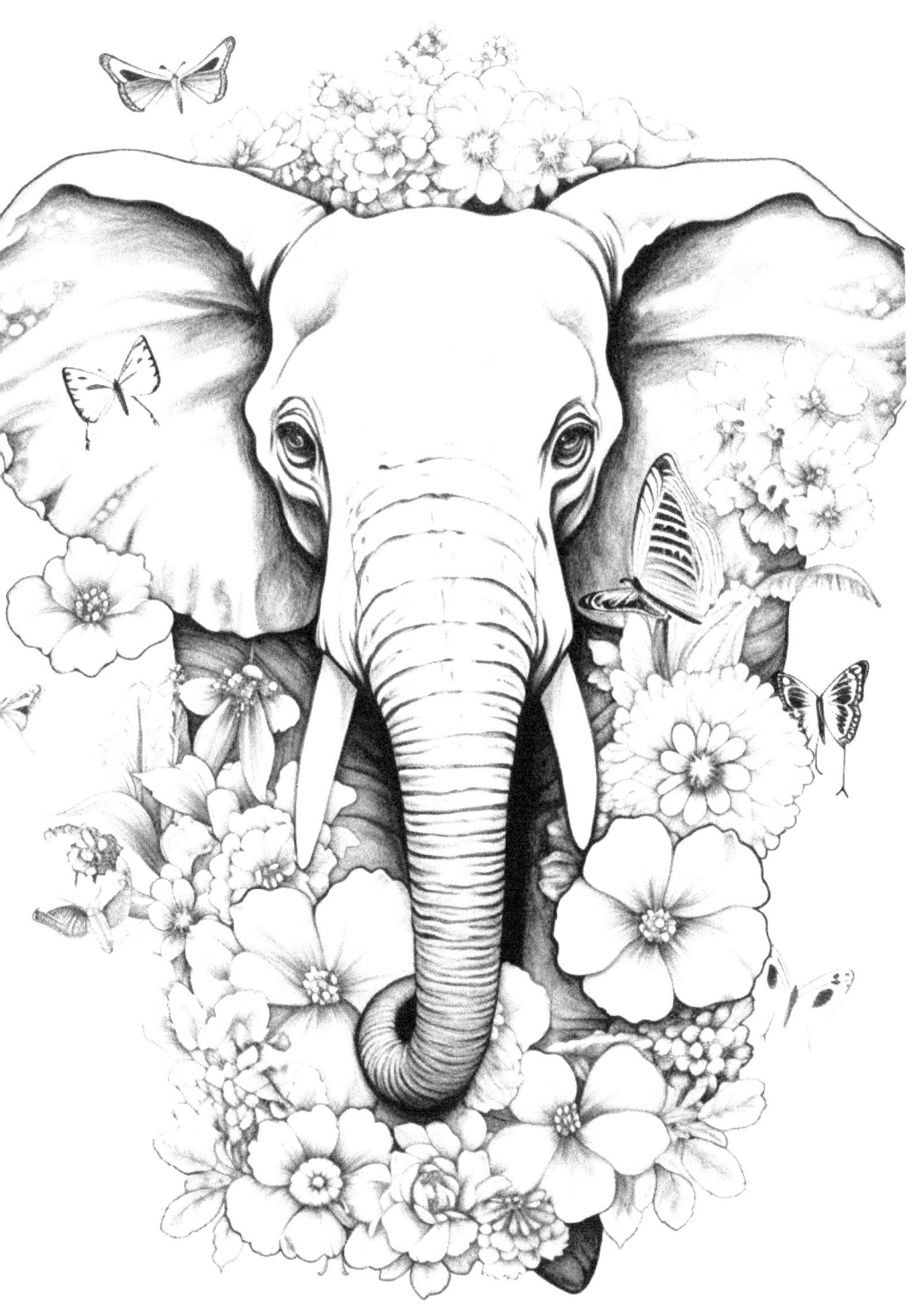

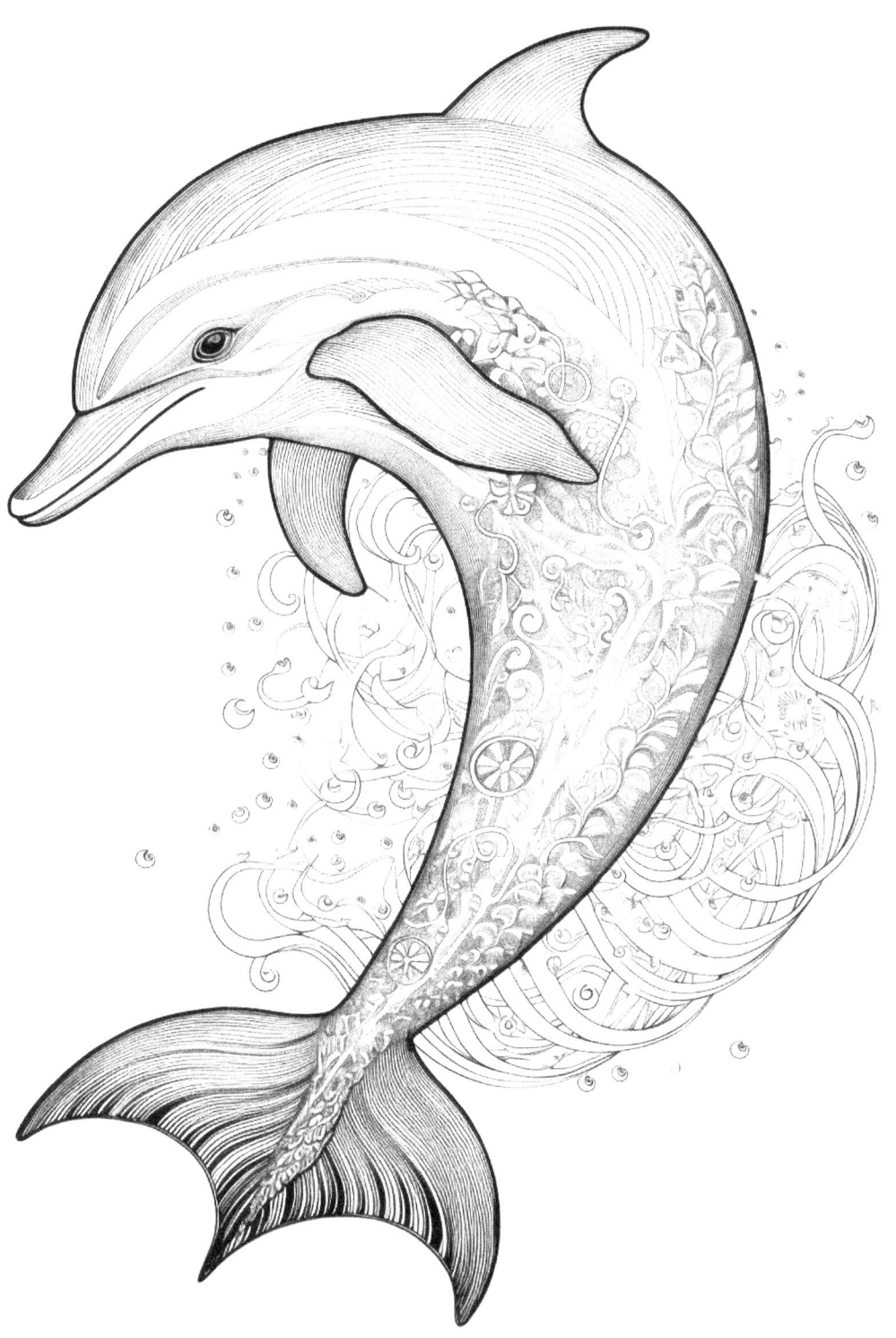

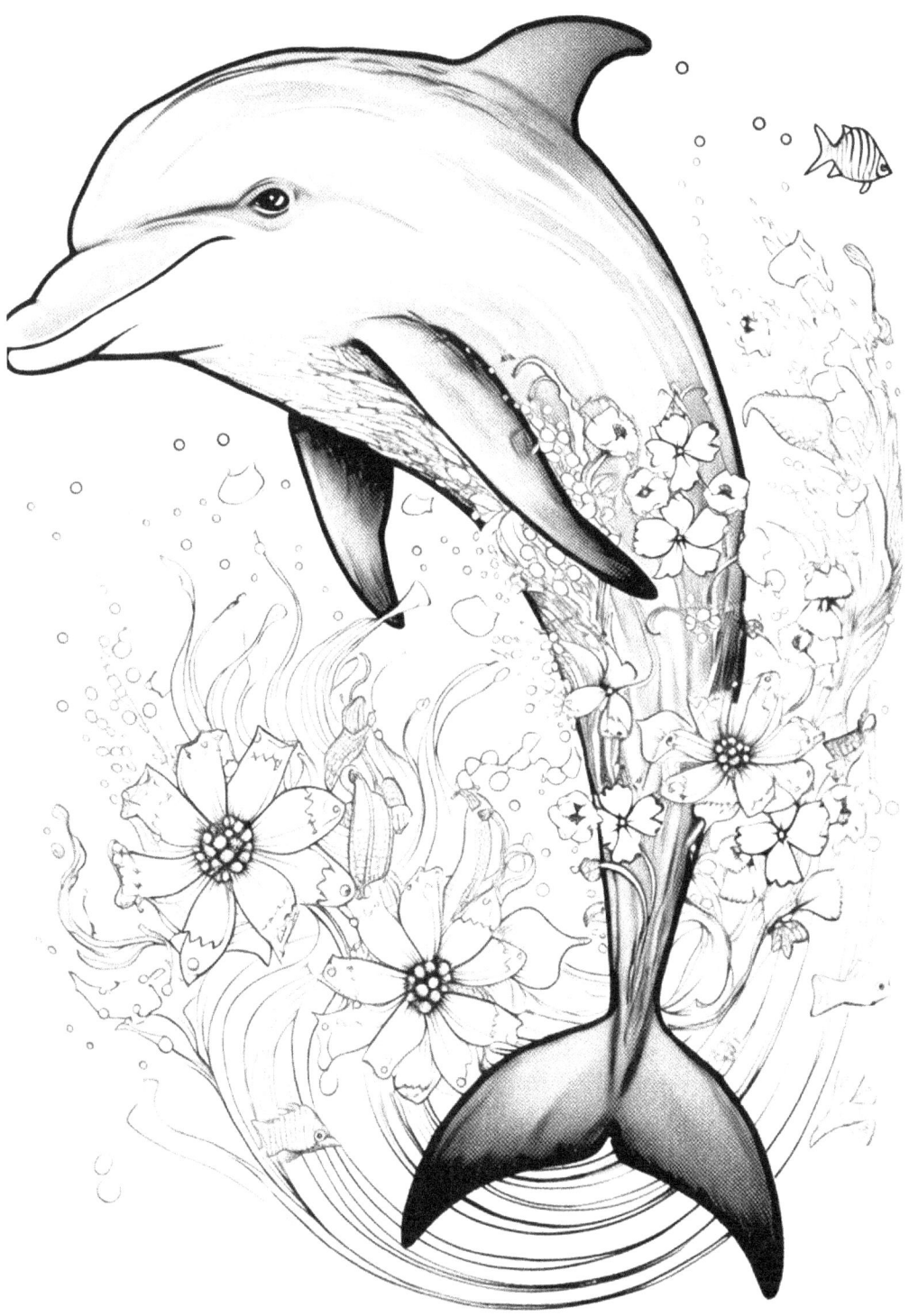

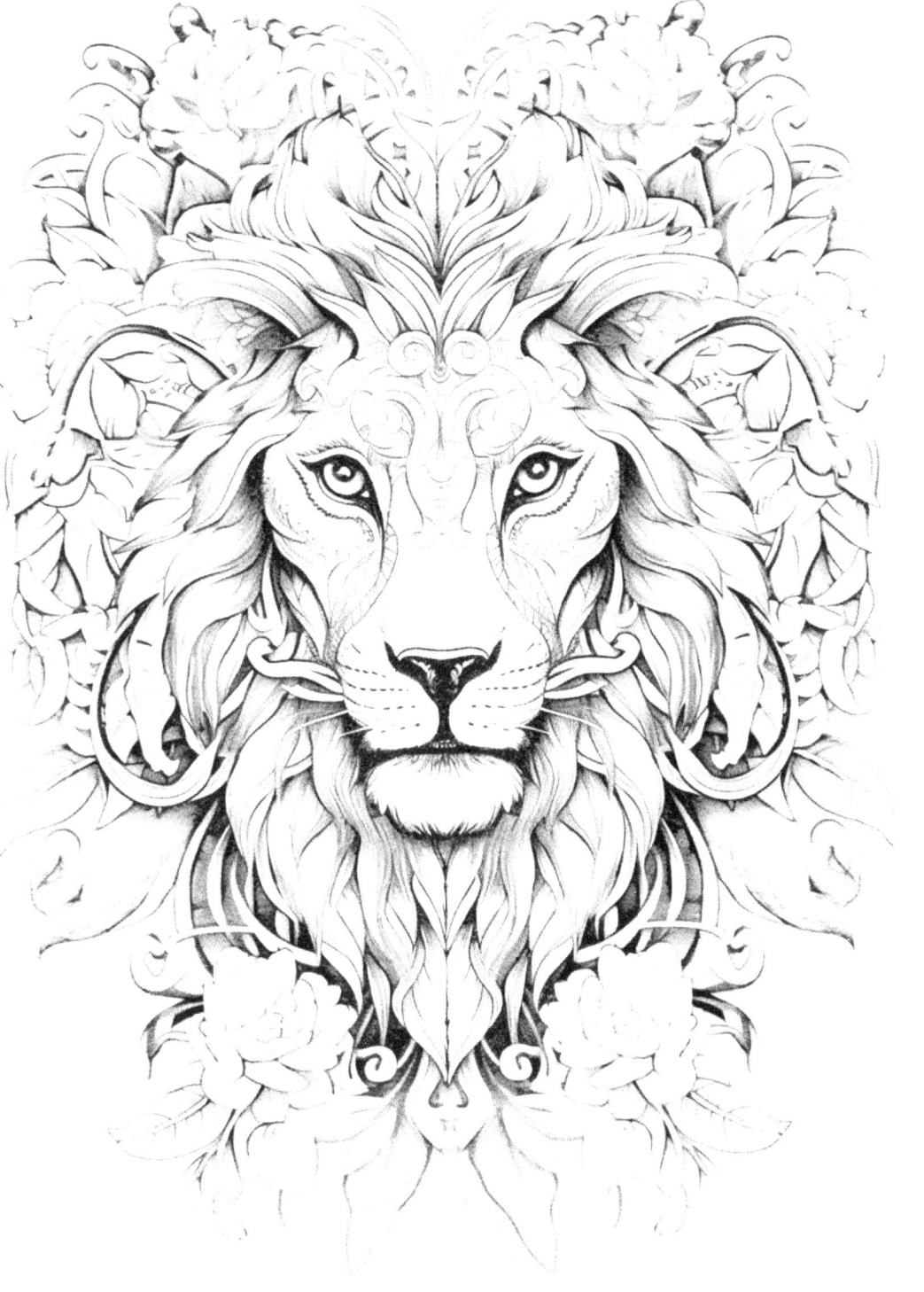

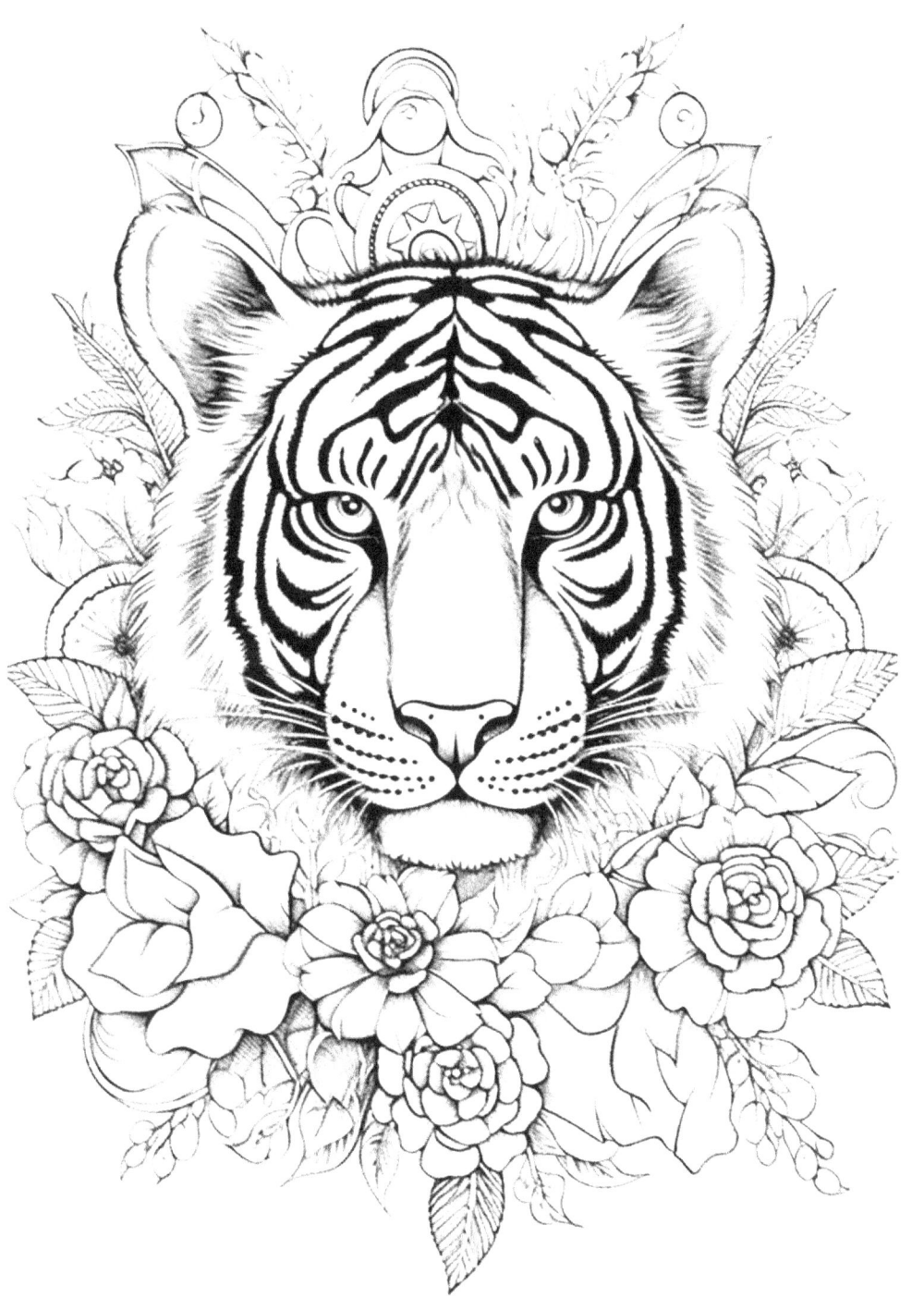

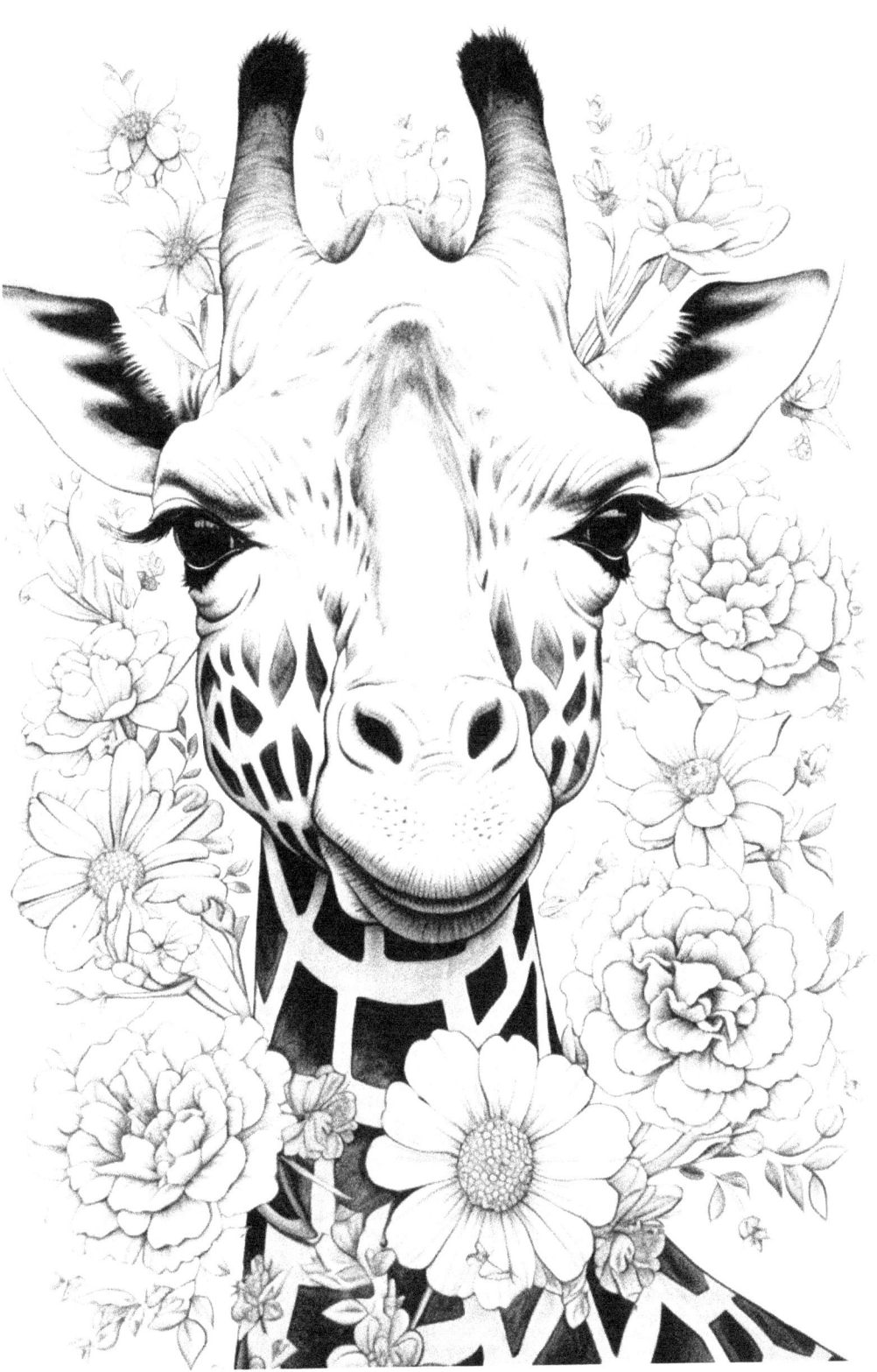

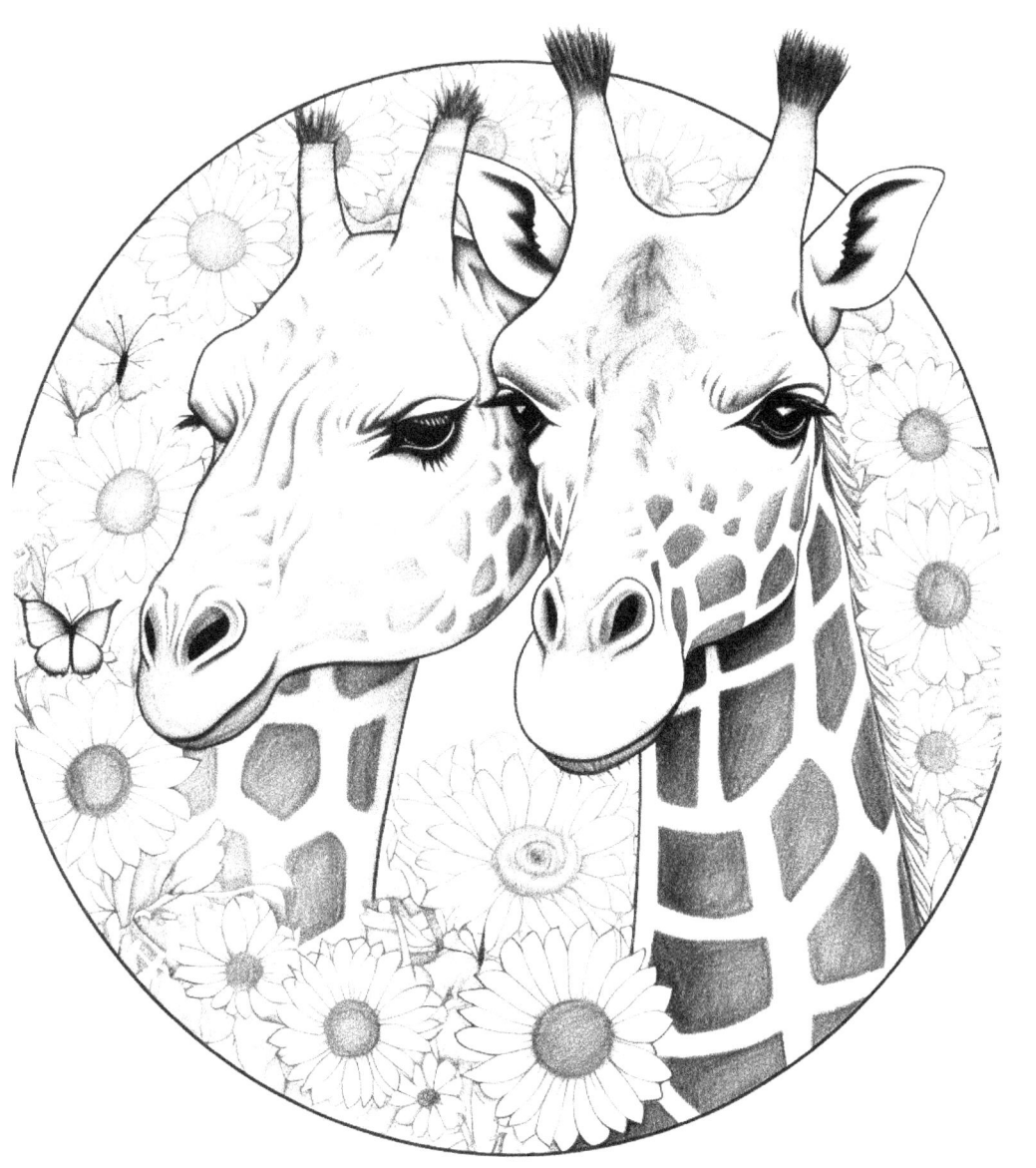

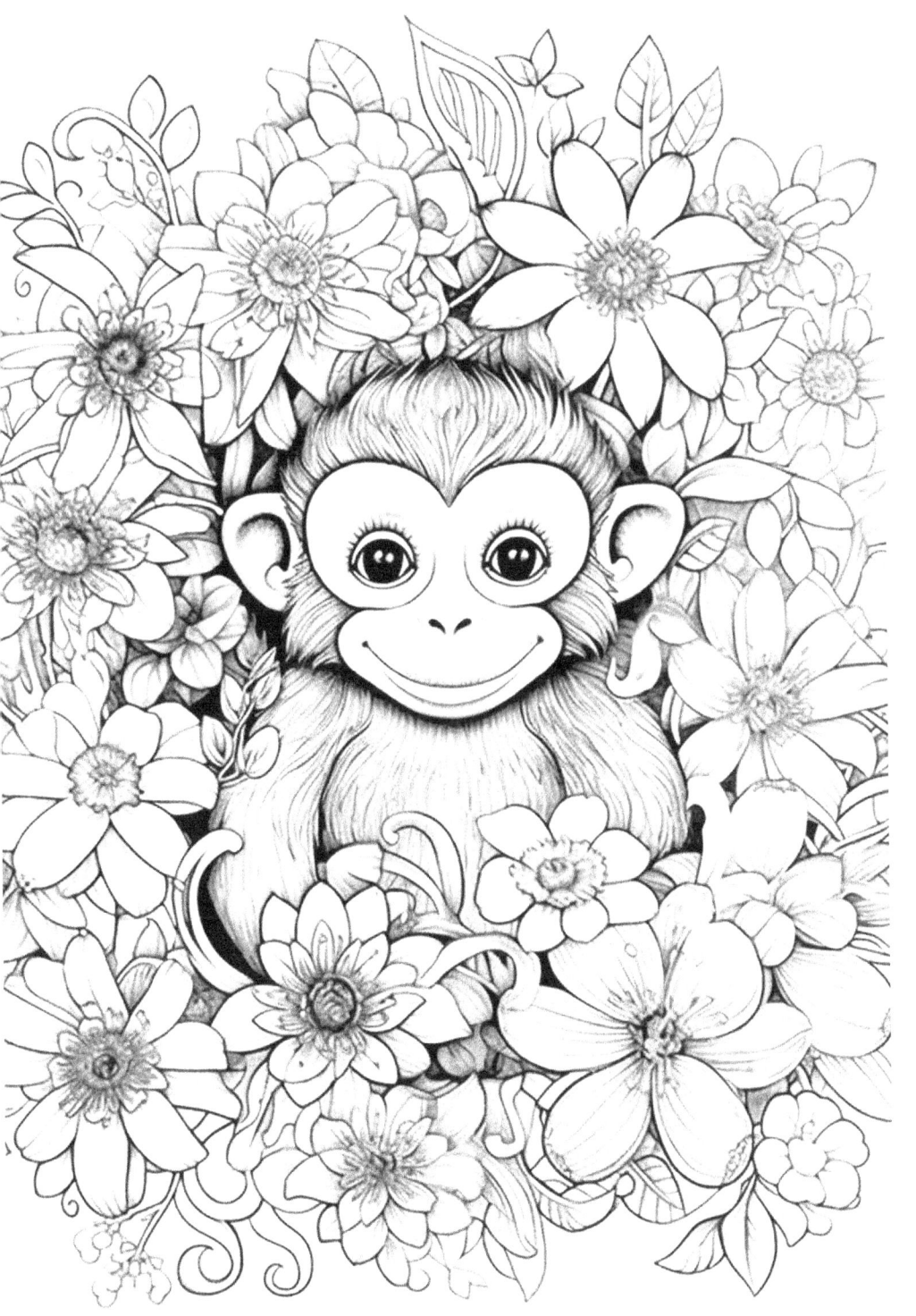

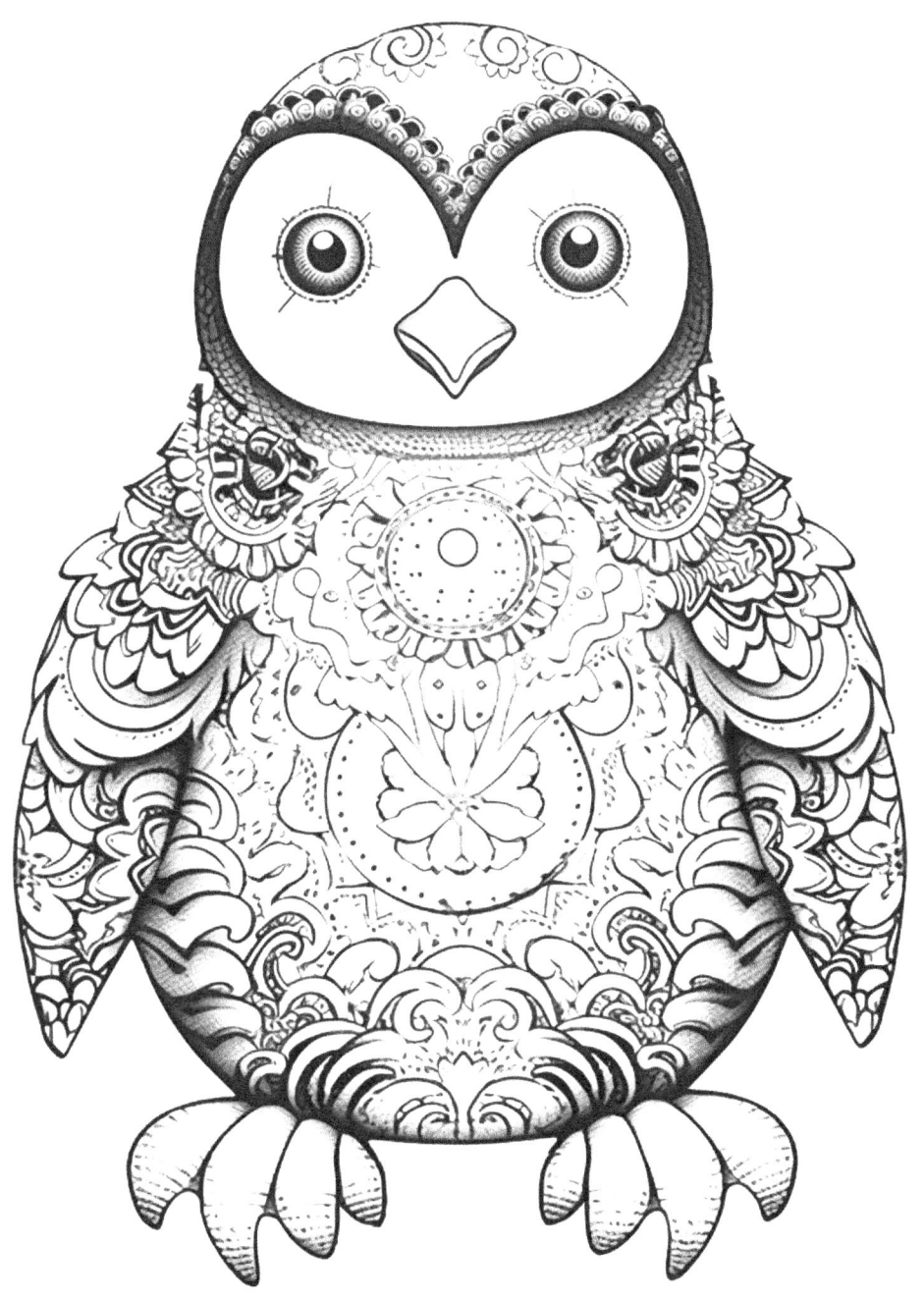

www.ingramcontent.com/pod-product-compliance
Lightning Source LLC
Chambersburg PA
CBHW070907220526
45466CB00005B/2159